Indie Rock Uke
by Andrew Driscoll

CD Contents

1	Tuning Notes	8	Street Strum
2	Middle of the Road	9	City Light
3	Big Break	10	Broken
4	Dark Pedal	11	Ten Seven Four
5	Soundtrack Seven	12	Planet Pattern
6	Koa Jam	13	Fast Strum
7	Power Uke	14	Indie Riff

1 2 3 4 5 6 7 8 9 0

© 2012 BY MEL BAY PUBLICATIONS, INC., PACIFIC, MO 63069.
ALL RIGHTS RESERVED. INTERNATIONAL COPYRIGHT SECURED. B.M.I. MADE AND PRINTED IN U.S.A.
No part of this publication may be reproduced in whole or in part, or stored in a retrieval system, or transmitted in any form
or by any means, electronic, mechanical, photocopy, recording, or otherwise, without written permission of the publisher.

Visit us on the Web at www.melbay.com — E-mail us at email@melbay.com

Table of Contents

Introduction 3
Righ Hand Technique 4
Ukulele Tuning 5
Ukulele Fretboard Diagram 6
Ukulele Chord Chart 7
   Middle of the Road 8
   Big Break 10
   Dark Pedal 12
   Soundtrack Seven 14
   Koa Jam 16
   Power Uke 18
   Street Strum 20
   City Light 22
   Broken 24
   Ten Seven Four 26
   Planet Pattern 28
   Fast Strum 30
   Indie Riff 34

Introduction

In recent years the ukulele has had a major resurgence in popularity. The ukulele is once again being heard in hit songs as well as all over the indie rock scene. Taylor Swift, Jason Mraz, and Eddie Vedder are examples of major artists whose music sometimes features the ukulele. The material in this book is designed to be a fun introduction to playing the ukulele in an acoustic rock or indie rock setting.

Before You Begin

The difficulty level of the material varies somewhat between the exercises as well as within the exercises themselves. Therefore, if you encounter something that is too difficult feel free to move on to another example. You can always return to the harder material later.

All of the examples are written in standard notation as well as ukulele tablature. Please note that in this book doubled notes are omitted from the standard notation. However, the doubling does appear in the tablature. For example:

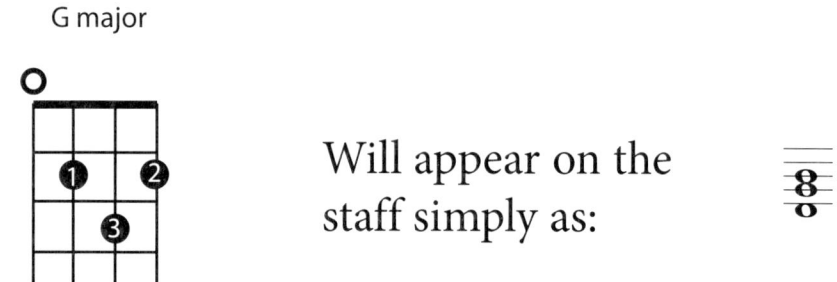

Right Hand Technique

The examples on the CD were recorded using a number of different ukulele strumming techniques. These include simply strumming the ukulele with the thumb or index finger; using the tops of the fingernails similar to a claw hammer banjo player; and fingerpicking the ukulele like a classical guitarist. Usually more than one of these techniques is suitable for playing any one of the examples. I encourage you to experiment with them all. They each have their own sonic character.

Ukulele Tuning

The examples in the book use standard C6 ukulele tuning. You can use the chart below along with a tuner, a piano or the first CD track to tune your ukulele.

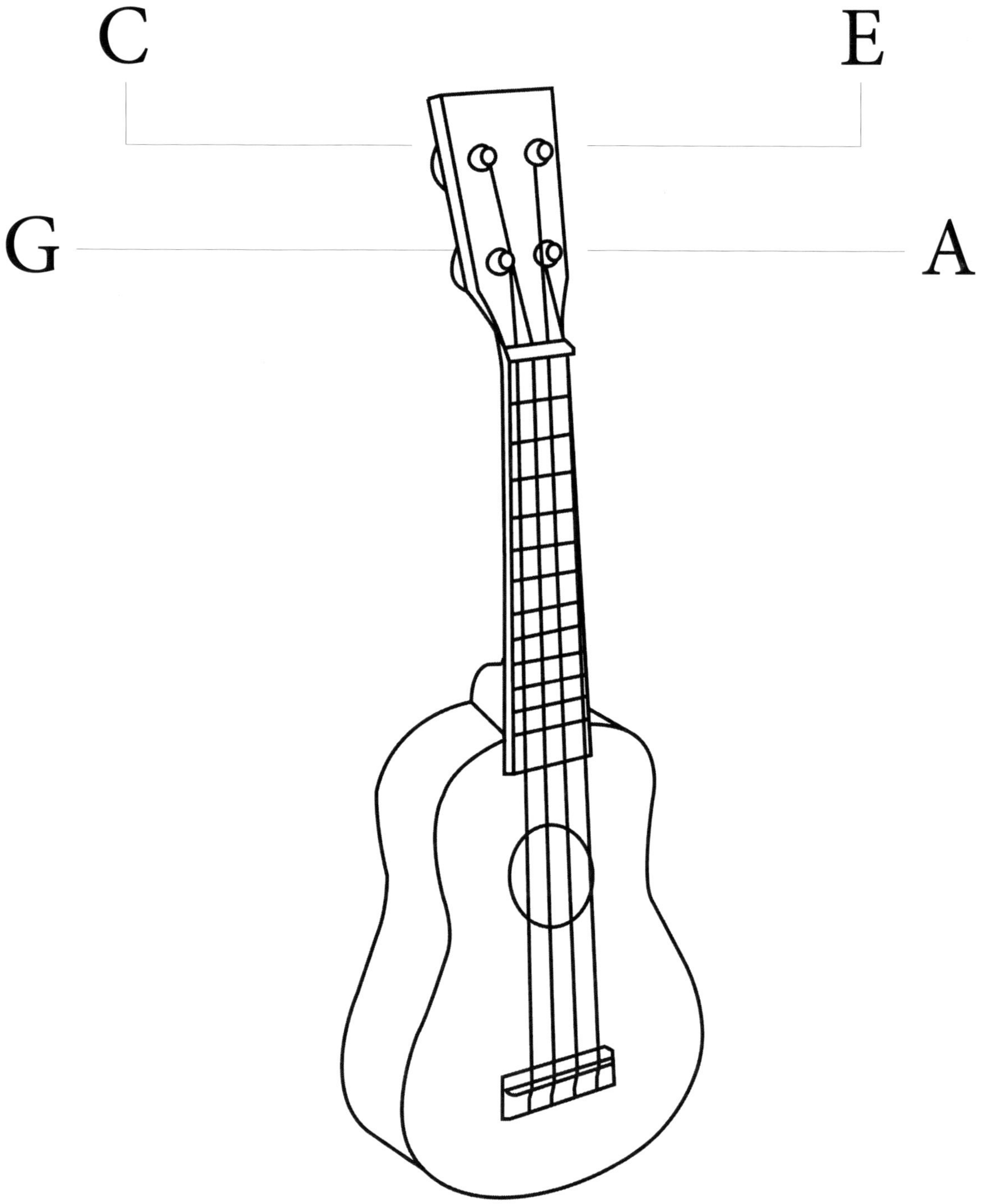

C   E

G   A

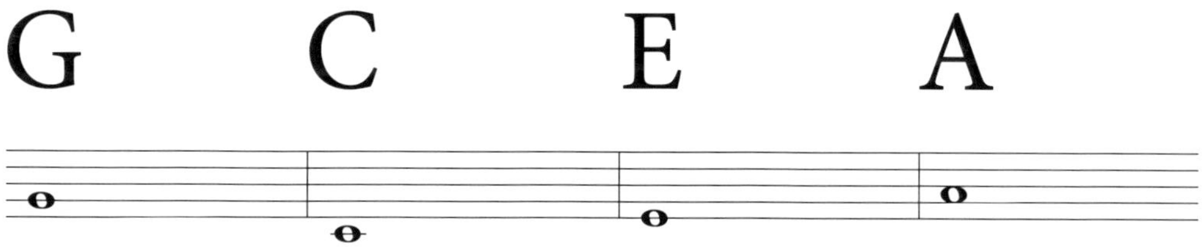

G   C   E   A

Ukulele Fretboard Diagram

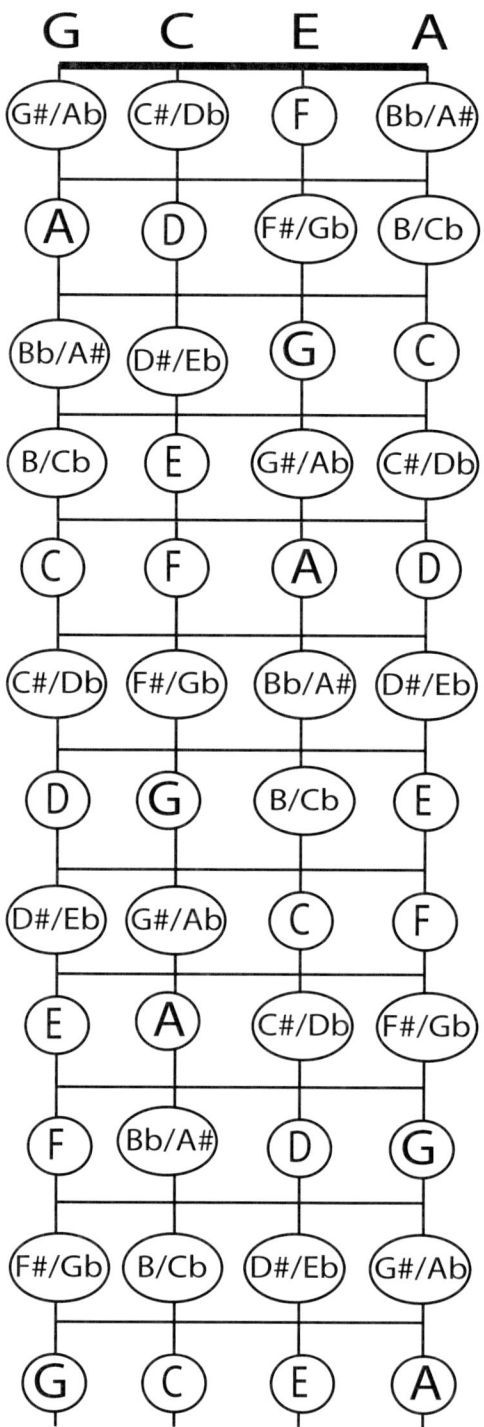

You can refer to the chart below for chords that are used in the examples.

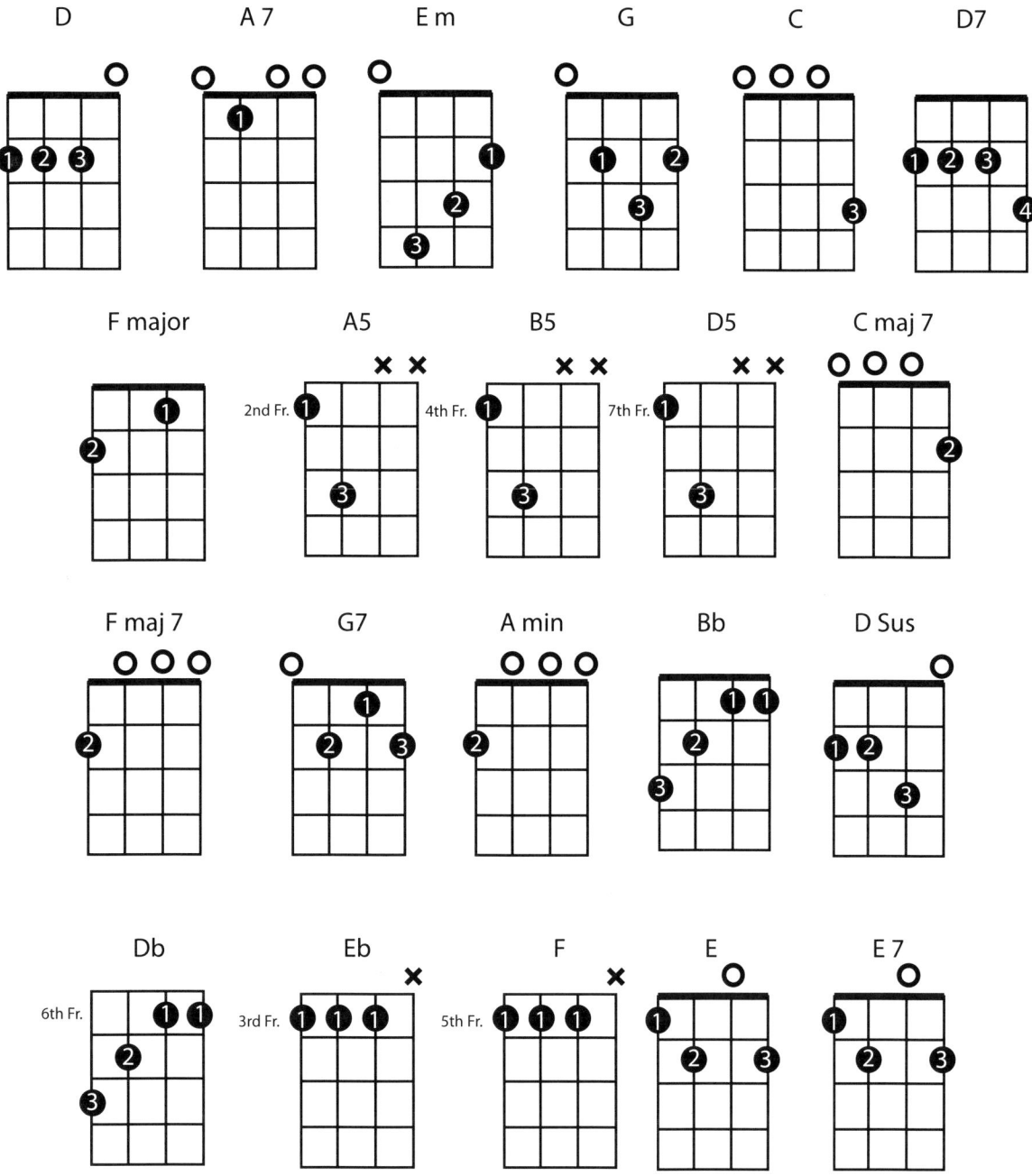

Middle of the Road

This page has been left blank
to avoid awkward page turns.

Big Break

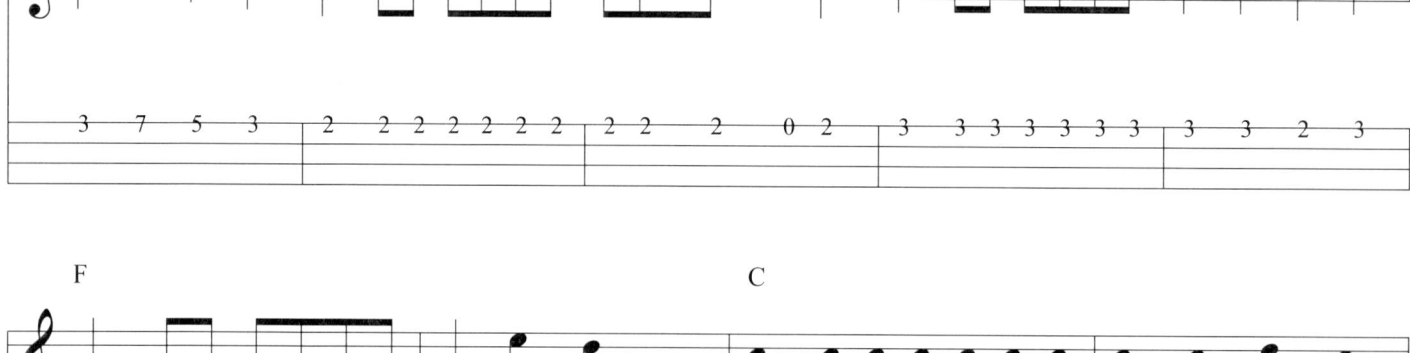
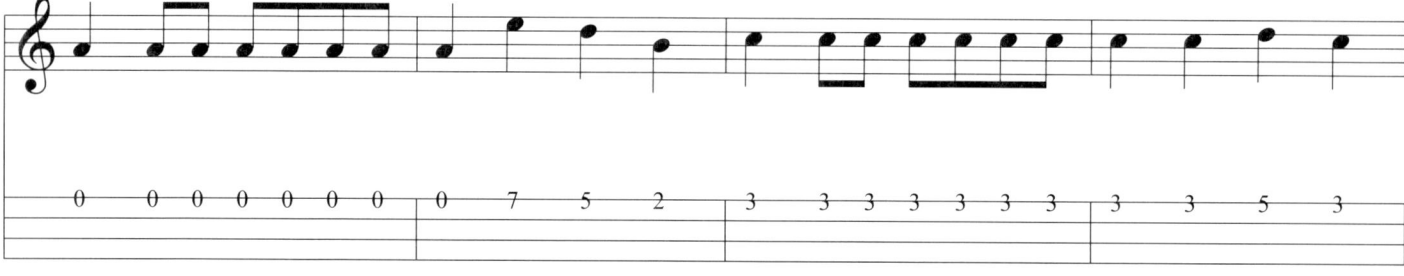

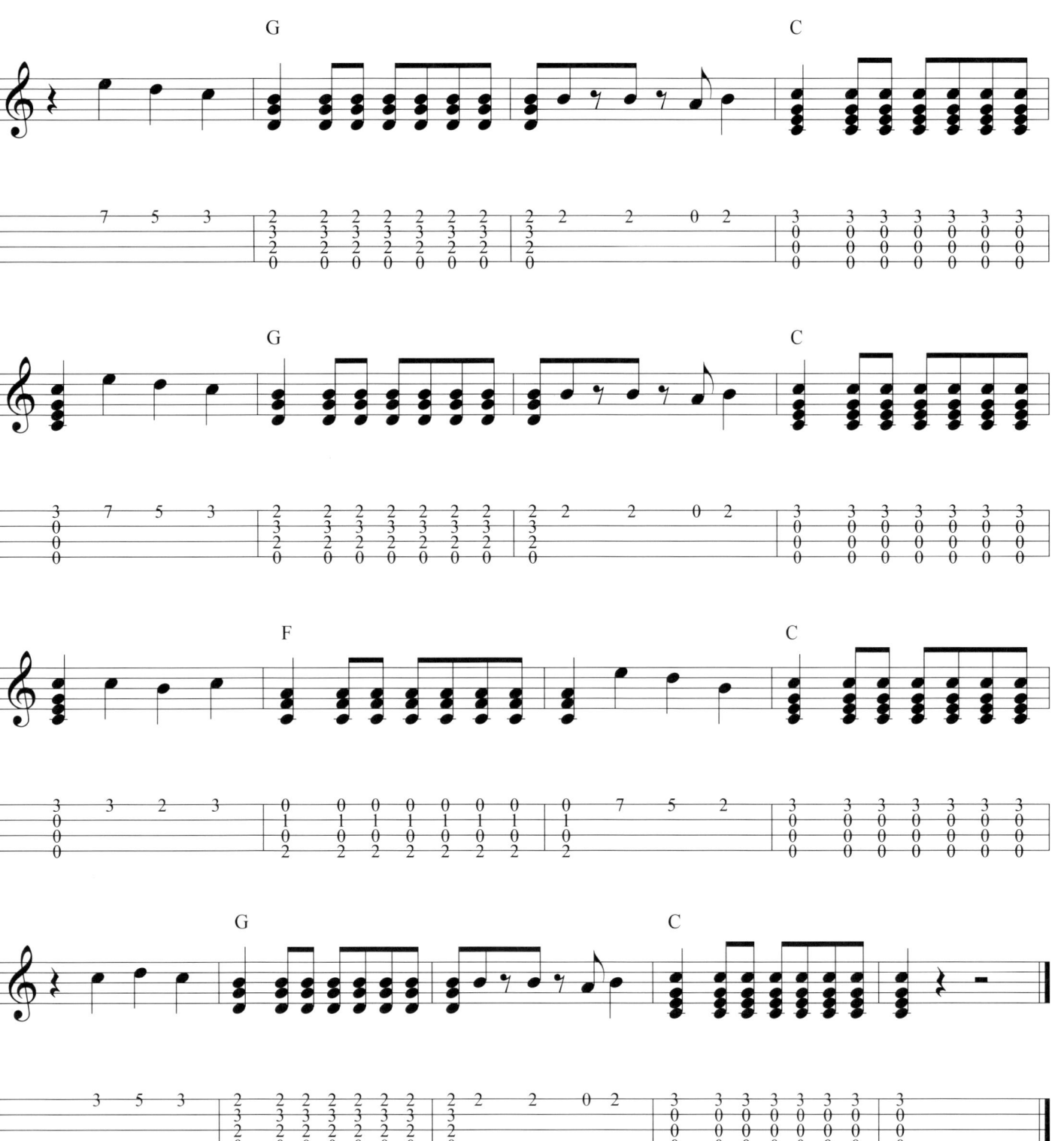

Dark Pedal

Soundtrack Seven

Koa Jam

Power Uke

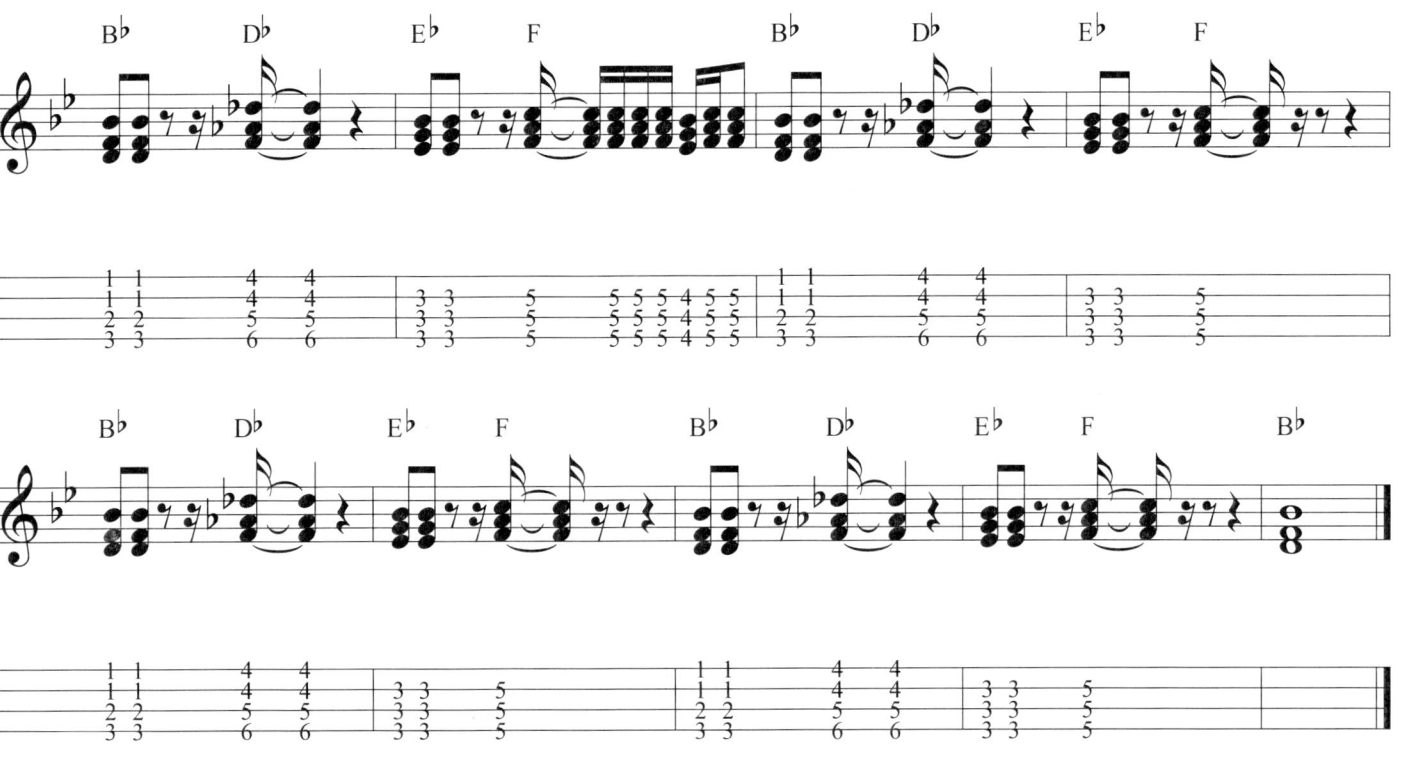

Street Strum

City Light

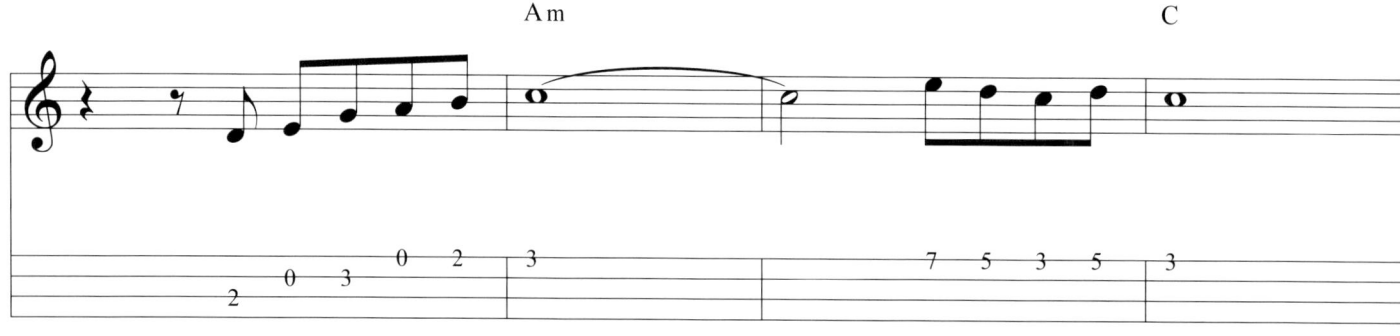
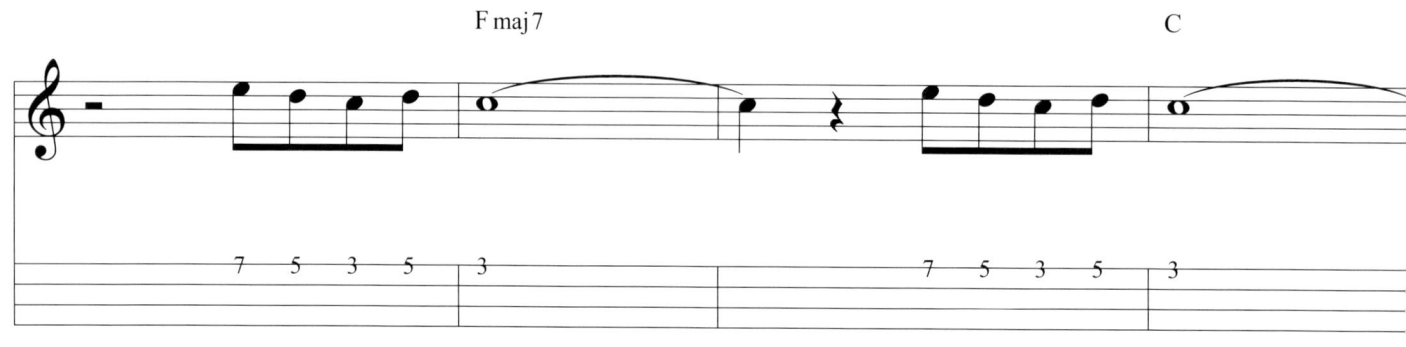

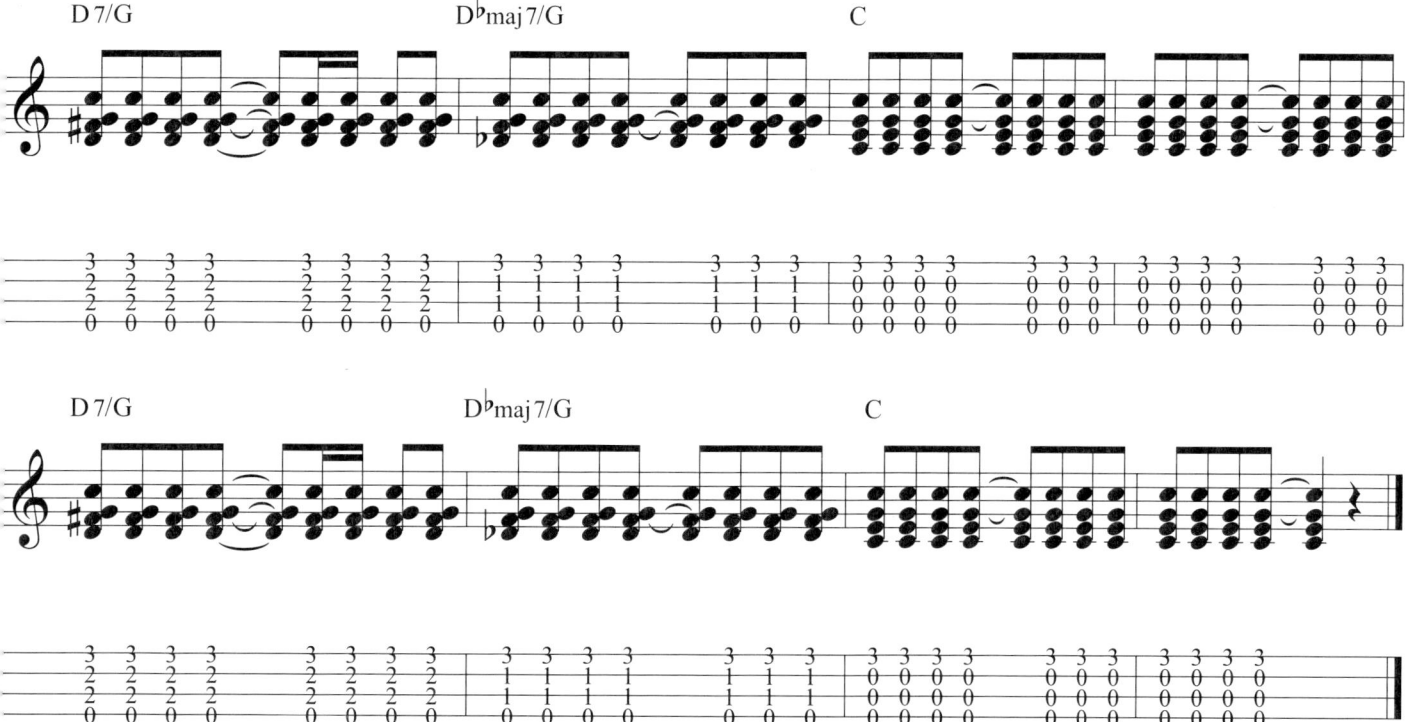

Broken

Ten Seven Four

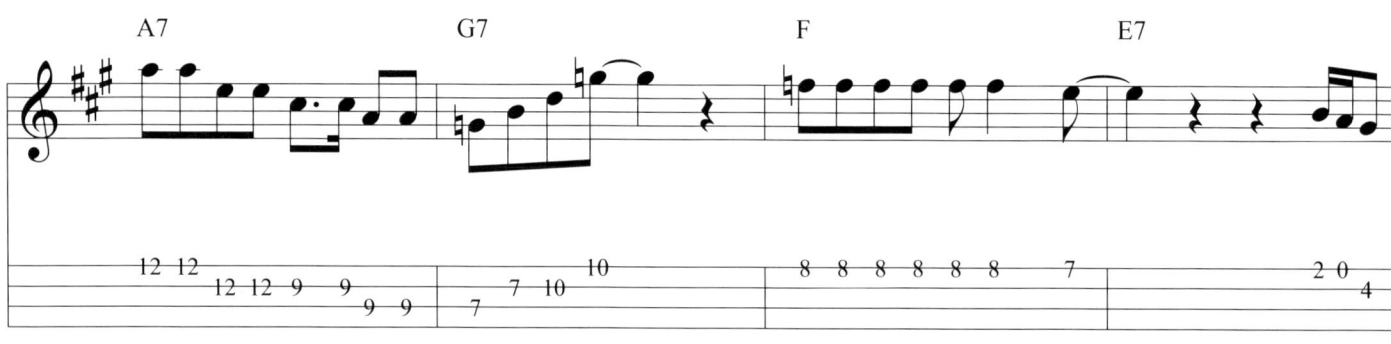

Planet Pattern

Fast Strum

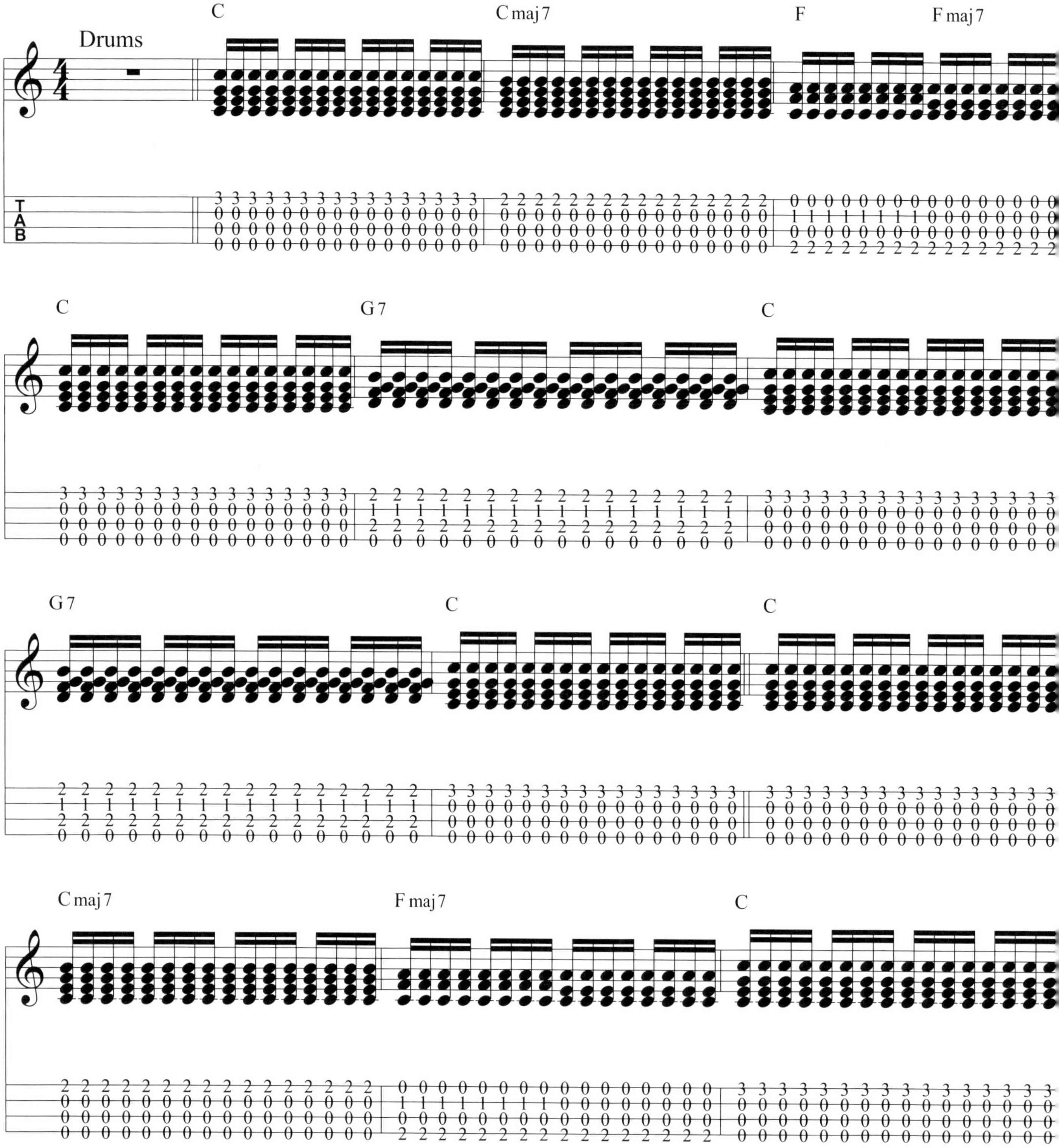

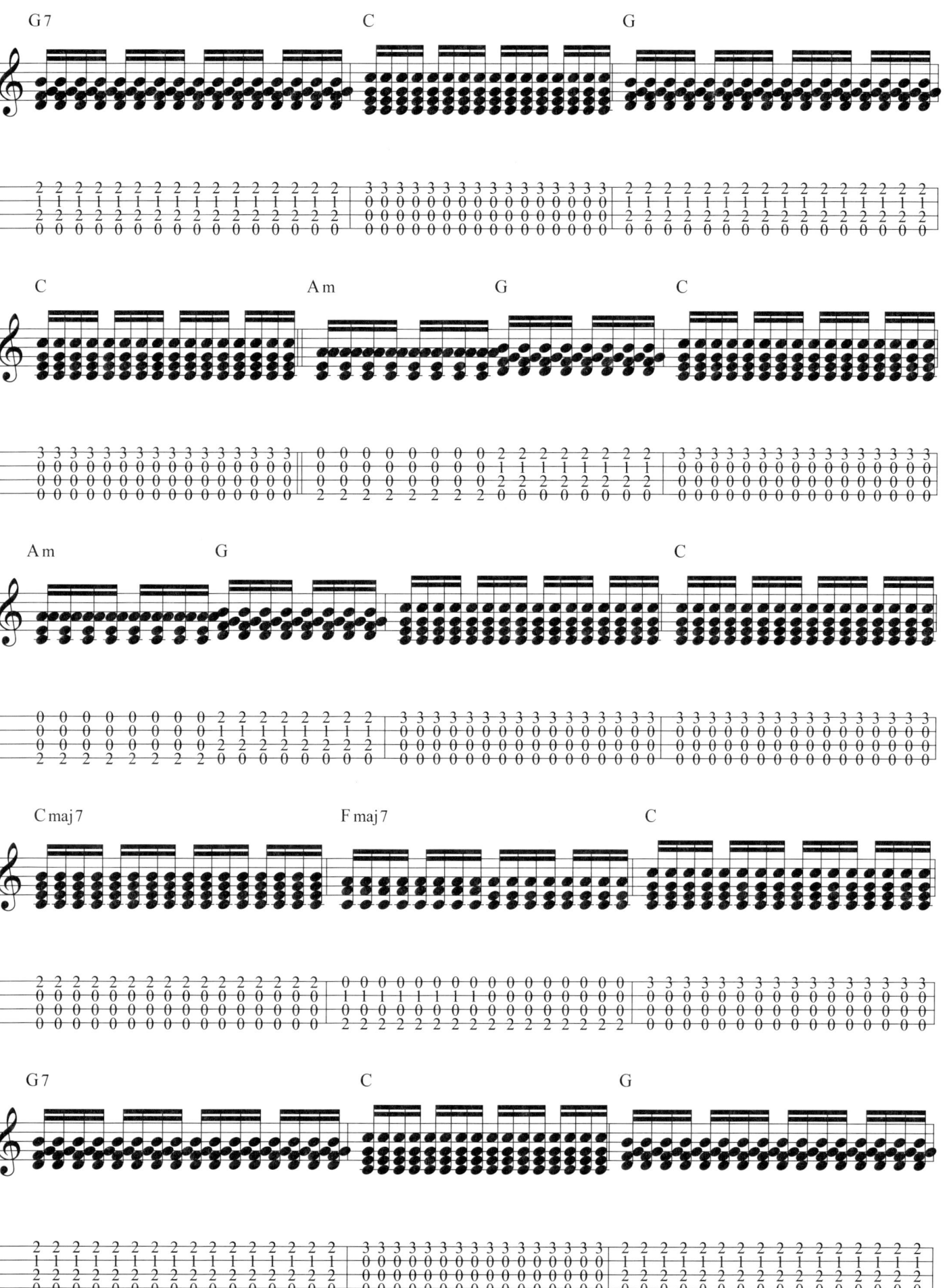

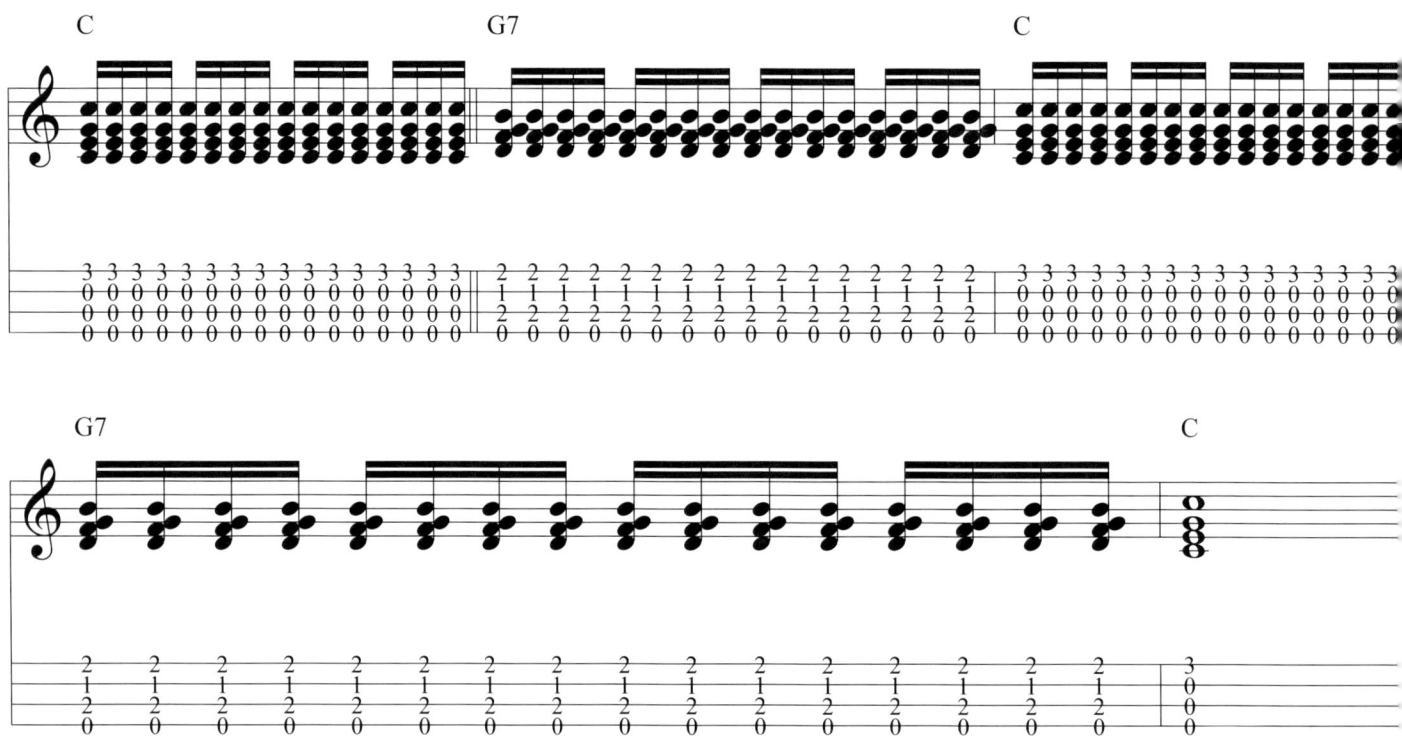

This page has been left blank to avoid awkward page turns.

Indie Riff

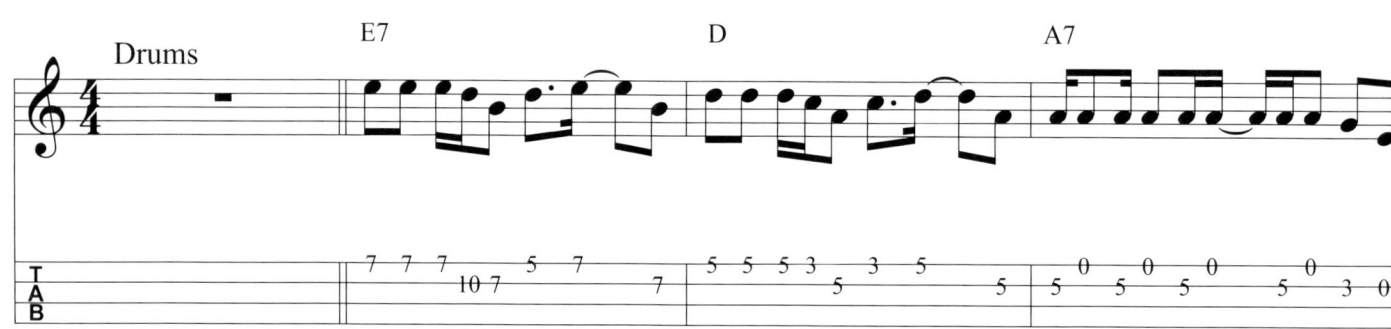